All Scripture references taken from the KJV of the Holy Bible, unless otherwise indicated.

Courts of Marriage: Prayers for Marriage in the Courts of Heaven

by Dr. Marlene Miles

Freshwater Press 2023

ISBN: 978-1-963164-07-7

Paperback Version

Table of Contents

Courts of Marriage:
Prayers for Marriage in the Courts of Heaven

This book is all prayer. Just pray it.

Repentance & Renunciation

Holy Spirit Fire fall.

Father, empower me to prevail in prayer in Jesus' Name. Lord, in the Name of Jesus I give my life to You. I dedicate, I rededicate my life to You. Please forgive me of all sins, sins of omission and commission. Give me a Godly sorrow for my sins and create a new spirit in me, in the Name of Jesus.

I believe that Jesus came to this Earth and He died for us, and on the third day You raised Him up, Father. He has taken our sins so that we may live. I believe in my heart that He is Lord, and I confess with my mouth, and I am saved, in the Name of Jesus. Amen.

Lord, I renounce every evil covenant and curse. I forsake all sin, and I resist the devil so he can flee from me. Lord, today I ask for Your Mercy and Your forgiveness over my sins and the sins of my ancestors, as well.

In the whole armor of God, I ask for protection against all evil *spirits* that would try to come against these prayers. Today we are praying about evil *spirits* that try to disrupt or block marriages.

Lord, empower these prayers to drive off anti-marriage and anti-Kingdom demons, in the Name of Jesus.

Lord, we thank You that Marriage is a divine purpose; and Lord, let us fulfill purpose, all to the praise of Your glory, in the Name of Jesus.

Lord, let us be fruitful and multiply according to Your order, in the context of marriage, in the Name of Jesus.

Lord, may Your order and process of marriage never be violated. If my ancestors have violated Your order and plan for marriage, Lord, I repent for them, in the Name of Jesus.

I break every curse of evil dedication. Lord, any garment or mark on me, or in me that is attracting anti-marriage *spirits* or marital failure *spirits*, be blotted out by the Blood of Jesus. Any mark due to faulty foundation or evil dedication be removed by the power in the Blood of Jesus.

I plead the Blood of Jesus. Amen.

Courts of the Lord

Lord, in the Name of Jesus, I enter into Your Gates with thanksgiving. I enter into Your Courts with praise. I praise You because You are worthy, You are righteous and just.

Father, thank You, and I enter into the Heavenly Courts asking for Mercy and I petition Your Grace and Your Mercy for my marital destiny, in the Name of Jesus.

I plead the Blood of Jesus. Lord, purify me that I may come before You, in the Name of Jesus. Anything that would hinder my petition, Lord, let it be removed, in Jesus' Name.

My own righteousness is as filthy rags, but Lord, wash me clean and give me proper attire to present before You. Lord, grant my petition for my divine marital destiny, in the Name of Jesus.

Have Mercy on me, Father, for we all have sinned and fallen short of the glory of God. Lord, look upon me with Mercy and forgive me of all iniquity, in the Name of Jesus.

Lord, I come to You clothed in my right mind and in my right garments, in the Name of Jesus. But if my garment needs to be changed, Lord, change it, in the Name of Jesus.

O Lord, deliver me from the repercussions of the sins of my ancestors. Protect me and my family from ancestral iniquity, in the Name of Jesus Christ, Amen.

Father, send forth divine deliverance from all ancestry, family, bloodline, and generational curses that are blocking my progress, and my marital destiny. Send it by the Blood of Jesus. Amen.

Son of David have Mercy upon me, in the Name of Jesus.

Blood of Jesus speak Mercy for me, in the Name of Jesus.

Jesus, thou Son of God have Mercy upon me, in the Name of Jesus.

Son of David, have Mercy upon me.

I need Mercy to answer every evil altar that is crying out against me, in the Name of Jesus.

King of kings, I thank You for Your Grace, in the Name of Jesus. God of Mercy, have Mercy on me and cover me with the garment of Mercy, in the Name of Jesus.

Let Your Mercy blot out the evil handwriting against my life, in the Name of Jesus.

I come into the Courts of Heaven to inquire about and answer any evil petition before the Thrones of God regarding my marital situation, my marriage, my life, my family, my children, in the Name of Jesus.

Father, I know if there is accusation against me before You at Your Throne of Mercy You would let me know. Regarding marriage, marital rights, sexual rights, are there accusations up against me at this Throne?

I ask to know who is accusing me, or has accused me, in the Name of Jesus.

Lord, have them bring forth the documents, all the documents, the hidden documents, any agreements, contracts, or certificates against me, in the Name of Jesus.

With Jesus as my Advocate I ask to see those documents and those accusations that are against me, in the Name of Jesus.

My Courtroom Plea

Yes, I am guilty, I have sinned against You. I have sinned against You, Lord. Forgive me, in the Name of Jesus.

I stand in authority for my bloodline – my bloodline has sinned against You, Lord. Forgive my parents, forgive my ancestors, in the Name of Jesus.

My defense is the Blood of Jesus. The Blood of Jesus. The Blood of Jesus. I plead the Blood of Jesus. It washes white as snow, it cleanses from all unrighteousness, it removes stains and iniquity because I am in Christ, now. I am in Christ, I am in Christ, I put on Christ, I plead the Blood, I plead the Blood of Jesus, in the Name of Jesus.

For Christ has redeemed us from the Curse of the Law. Every curse that has blocked or hindered me from marriage, staying married and being happy in marriage with my God-ordained Kingdom spouse, let every curse be broken, today, in the Name of Jesus.

Every generational curse in my family that has stopped my family members from finding their Kingdom spouse, marrying and staying married and being happy and successful in marriage with a Kingdom spouse, Lord, let every generational curse be broken today by Heavenly decree from Your Throne of Grace and Mercy, in the Name of Jesus.

Father, every **witchcraft curse** that has been working against my marital life, I ask You that the power of that witchcraft curse be broken over my life and marital destiny, today, in the Name of Jesus.

Lord, whoever is occupying my place of marriage and destiny, Lord Jesus, remove them, in the Name of Jesus.

Anti-Marriage Curses

My head, reject every word of delay, of misfortune, of failure, and stagnation, in the Name of Jesus.

I break the power of every negative pronouncement, enchantment, curse, divination, spell, and incantation released upon me through evil family and foundational curses, in the Name of Jesus.

I break and scatter every curse of marital delay affecting my family of birth, the family of my father's house, in Jesus' Name.

I break and release myself, from every evil dedication and collective evil covenant, in the Name of Jesus.

Blood of Jesus, Holy Ghost Fire put a hedge of protection around me from evil dedication and altars that are emanating against me, in the Name of Jesus.

By Holy Ghost Fire, I break and destroy every destructive covenant operating in my life, in the Name of Jesus.

Blood of Jesus Christ, break and release me from every covenant with the *idols* of my father's house in my foundation, in the Name of Jesus.

By the Fire of Heaven, I break and release myself from every covenant with idols of my bloodline, in the Name of Jesus.

Anti-marriage spells and curses—I break every spell that has hindered the destiny of my family from being saved, living saved, staying saved, and being also effective in Christ, in ministry, in purpose, and in marriage, in the Name of Jesus.

Let every spell resisting my Kingdom marriage be broken now, in the Courts of Heaven today, in the Name of Jesus.

Whatever spell the enemy is using to hold the marital destiny of my family hostage, I break it, I break it, I break it! Let it be broken in the Courts of Heaven today, in the Name of Jesus.

No incantation can work against Jacob; I am in Jacob. I am in Israel - by adoption and by the grafting in, in the Name of Jesus.

I break the power of every anti-marriage spell cast against me, my family, my bloodline, and ask that the entity coming against us lose that power, lose the power, lose all power against me and against my family, in the Name of Jesus.

Lord, You are angry with the wicked every day – let my enemies fall into judgment with You. Let them fall into the hands of an angry God; judge the wicked that are up against me, in the Name of Jesus.

Lord, overturn and make an end to the spells, hexes, vexes, curses, incantations, black magic, white magic, green magic, red magic, and evil judgments from covens and satanic courts against me, in the Name of Jesus.

Thank You, Lord for hearing my petitions today and answering, and for setting me free, for setting my family free, and my bloodline free, and free indeed, in the Name of Jesus.

Foundation

Lord, in the Name of Jesus, break the hold the enemy has on my foundation, my family, my bloodline, myself, and my marital destiny, in the Name of Jesus.

Lord, if You have been looking for one to free this family in Jesus Christ, I am the one – use me Lord, as Your Battle Axe to repair the faulty foundation of my family, in Jesus' Name.

Every foundational problem from both sides of my family that is blocking or stealing my blessings, be burned to ashes, in the Name of Jesus.

Lord, close every dimensional access point the enemy has into my life and my family's lives; repair our faulty foundation, in the Name of Jesus Christ.

Holy Ghost Fire, destroy every evil *monitoring spirit* and their respective devices that are spying on me, my family, and/or my business, in the Name of Jesus.

Every evil secret working against me, and my family be exposed and scattered, in the Name of Jesus.

Lord, let the troublers of my life and family be troubled, and be disgraced, in the Name of Jesus.

Oh Lord, let the hiding places that the enemy has found; let the enemy be found out. Let the Light of God, shine brightly on them that they scatter like roaches, in the Name of Jesus.

I (your name) ________ come against every evil hand and, every evil tongue, *spirit*, power, and entity raised to trouble my peace and my family, in the Name of Jesus. I strike you with blindness. Die, in the Name of Jesus.

Father in Heaven, remove all iniquity from past sins found in the foundation of my father's house, that is affecting me now, in the Name of Jesus.

Ancient altars of my bloodline, that I know nothing about, that are still emanating against me and my generations, be cut off, be cut off, be cut off, in the Name of Jesus. Seize up and cease operation against me, in Jesus' Name. Amen.

Ancient family altars receiving sacrifices and manipulating my life, receive Fire, receive Fire, receive Fire, Holy Ghost Fire, receive Fire, and burn to ashes, in Jesus' Name.

Any *idol* or river that I have been dedicated to when I was a baby, release me by Fire and die, in the Name of Jesus.

I break any ancestral curse and covenant following me about, in Jesus' Name.

Strange hands and legs tying down my foundation, I come against you, I come against you, with the Fire of the Holy Ghost, receive the Fire of Judgment, in the Name of Jesus.

Family idols crying against my breakthroughs, break! Break! by the Blood of Jesus.

Fire Quake of God, destroy the ancestral prison holding me captive, in Jesus' Name.

I release myself from every evil domination, control, and captivity, in the Name of Jesus.

Anything programmed into my life, especially such as using the *Triangular Powers*, or any element, to make me suffer the way people are suffering in my family, I cancel it by the Blood of

Jesus. I cancel it by the power in the Blood of Jesus.

Innocent blood shed by my ancestors, crying against my destiny, be silenced by the Blood of Jesus.

Fire of deliverance; destroy every battle over my blood, in the Name of Jesus.

Blood of Jesus, deliver me from generational and ancestral battles, in the Name of Jesus.

Lord, arise and attack every evil power attacking me with curses, in Jesus' Name. I hide myself and my destiny in the Blood of Jesus Christ. Amen.

By the authority given to me to tread on every serpent and scorpion, I break and release myself from every evil covenant my parents have put me in whether knowingly or unknowingly, in Jesus' Name.

Blood of Jesus, break and release me from every soul tie, blood covenant and sexual covenant, in the Name of Jesus.

Holy Ghost Fire, break and release me from every evil covenant operating between me and my place of birth, in the Name of Jesus.

I cover and soak myself and my foundation with the Blood of Jesus Christ.

Every secret evil covenant working against me, Holy Ghost Fire, destroy them, in the Name of Jesus.

Evil and unfortunate familial inherited patterns, I break you, in the Name of Jesus.

O Lord, deliver me by Fire from every ancestral curse that I have been initiated into—destroy every evil initiation that involves me, in Jesus' Name.

Any family member or other relative who has stolen my blessings--, I retrieve them back now, in Jesus' Name.

All inherited infirmities and sicknesses in my body due to evil flow, dry up and die, in the Name of Jesus.

O Lord Jesus! Let Your Blood wash away every satanic pronouncement that has been pronounced over my life, even the ones I have made, myself, knowingly or unknowingly that is working against my life in the Name of Jesus.

Name

Father, uproot all curses and their consequences that have been linked to my name. Lord, if I have an evil name, change my name, change it by Fire, in the Name of Jesus.

With the Blood of Jesus, I myself free from every evil flow from my foundation, in Jesus' Name.

Every curse of *like father like son* and *like mother like daughter*--, collective bondage, break, break, and die, in the Name of Jesus.

Blood of Jesus Christ break and scatter every curse my parents have placed upon my life, in the Name of Jesus.

Every curse issued on my head from my father's house; die, in the Name of Jesus. I release myself from the strongholds of my father's house, in the Name of Jesus.

Any evil soul tie between me and anyone, break by the Fire of the Holy Ghost. Amen.

Generational Curses

Lord, I call on You to break every generational curse that is exerting power over me and the events of my life. in Jesus' Name.

Father, protect me and my family from every evil family curse assigned to destroy our lives, in Jesus' Name.

Father, whatever is in me that allows a curse to alight – I don't want it. Deliver me, Lord. Deliver me. Holy Spirit, You are the Spirit of Deliverance– deliver me, in the Name of Jesus.

I break every evil yoke, every bondage, that the curses have placed today. and I break them by Fire. Lord, destroy them and scatter them all, in Jesus' Name.

Household witchcraft against my marital future and destiny, against my Kingdom spouse, against me, and my wedded bliss – stand down, stand down, or receive the wrath of God, in the Name of Jesus.

Witchcraft Curses

I use the Blood of Jesus to revoke and dismantle, deprogram, and scatter all evil magic covenants spells and chants, incantations, all anti-marriage curses, all marriage-failure curses.

I bind all covenants, spells, chants, incantations, yokes, and bondages working against me, and my marriage in the Name of Jesus.

Every enchantment or divination invoked against me, be destroyed by Holy Ghost Fire, in Jesus' Name.

Every shrine where my name, image or likeness is invoked, or used, I command them wiped out by Fire, in the mighty Name of Jesus Christ.

Every curse pronounced against my destiny, or against my family line, BREAK, in the Name of Jesus.

Every curse militating against my prosperity and the fulfilment of my goals, be destroyed, in the Name of Jesus.

Every barrier of limitation assigned against me, scatter now, in Jesus' Name.

Blood of Jesus, wipe away every bewitchment from me, from my head, my hands, my legs, every organ of my body, my life, my marriage, from all certificates with my name on them, in the Name of Jesus.

Father, burn to ashes, every witchcraft monitoring device used to monitor my progress and my life, in the Name of Jesus.

Every seat of witchcraft in my house and body receive fire, Receive Fire, receive Fire, and burn to ashes, in Jesus Name.

Witchcraft curses used on any area of my life, receive Fire, burn to ashes, roast to ashes, in the Name of Jesus.

Holy Ghost Fire, crush to pieces every witchcraft curse in the way of my life, my ministry, my purpose, my destiny, and my marital bliss, in the Name of Jesus.

Witchcraft curses of untimely death and poverty upon my life, break, in the Name of Jesus, and I return them to sender.

Witchcraft, curses of hardship upon my life, Break and scatter, in Jesus Name.

Any part of my life or destiny, arrested by witchcraft receive the power of God, and resurrection now, in Jesus' Name.

Lord Jesus let blessings and favor locate me everywhere I go, in Jesus' Name.

Every joint effort of witches and wizards against my life and family, Lord God, locate them, now. Burn them to ashes, in the Name of Jesus.

Strange curses hunting after my family, your time is up, DIE, in the Name of Jesus.

I declare: *No weapon formed against me shall prosper in the Name of Jesus.* Lord, let all evil giants on the mountain of my life, scatter, and die. Let them fall like Goliath, in the Name of Jesus.

I break every Satanic stronghold over my life, in the Name of Jesus.

Anything planted at my threshold to demote me, to harm me, to hurt me, be neutralized by Fire, in Jesus' Name.

Every stronghold attached to my breakthrough, I bind you, in Jesus' Name. Generational yokes of sorrow and weeping that are in my foundation, die, in the Name of Jesus.

Any strong man in my family that is keeping my breakthrough locked away, release them now, and die, in Jesus' Name.

Lord, You have power over everything. Glory to Your Name, Lord. Amen.

God of Mercy, have Mercy on me and cover me with a garment of Mercy, in the Name of Jesus.

Blood of Jesus, Holy Ghost, by Your power, purify my foundation, in the Name of Jesus.

Any form of witchcraft deeply rooted in my family--, Fire of God, Fire Axe of God go to the roots and destroy them, burn them, burn them out, in the Name of Jesus.

Any power assigned to pull me down, Die, in the Name of Jesus.

Every evil serpent in my life. Black serpent, Brown Serpent, White serpent, Green serpent, Red serpent, any serpent. Any evil serpent designed to waste the destiny of myself or my children, due to envy and jealousy, die in the Name of Jesus.

Powers that have vowed to keep me like this, be wasted by Fire, in Jesus' Name.

God of Elijah, rise in Your power, set me free from strange attacks, in the Name of Jesus.

Every arrow of affliction fired into my life to waste time and money and energy, backfire, in the Name of Jesus.

Any evil personality manipulating my life, confess and run mad, in Jesus' Name.

My family glory, hear the Word of the Lord, appear by Fire, in the Name of Jesus. My family glory, appear! In the Name of Jesus.

Envious witchcraft that causes people not to marry in my family, be dismantled, in Jesus' Name.

Let my breakthrough battle my enemies, in the Name of Jesus.

I command you witches and warlocks, by the authority in Christ to remove your hands from my life, by the power in the Blood of Jesus, the Blood of Jesus, the Blood of Jesus.

Any witchcraft rat, lizard, bird or cat assigned to shut down my blessings, die by Fire, die by Fire, die by Fire, in Jesus' Name.

Holy Ghost Fire destroy the foundation of delay and failure in my life, in Jesus' Name.

God arise and expose the evil personality waging war against me and my family, in Jesus' Name.

Blood of Jesus Christ, wipe away every bewitchment from my head, hands and certificates, in Jesus' Name.

Fire of God, burn to ashes every witchcraft monitoring gadget used to monitor my progress, in Jesus' Name.

Every seed of witchcraft in my house and body, receive Fire, receive Fire, and burn to ashes, in Jesus' Name.

Witchcraft curses used on any area of my life, receive Fire, burn to ashes, in Jesus' Name.

Holy Ghost Fire, crush to pieces every witchcraft curse operating in my life, in the Name of Jesus.

Every joint effort of witches and wizards against my life and family, let the Fire of God scatter them now, in the Name of Jesus Christ.

Strange curses hunting after my family, and at all costs, your assignment is over, be destroyed now, in the Name of Jesus of Nazareth.

I declare that no weapon formed against my life, or formed against me shall ever prosper in Jesus' Name. All evil giants on the mountain of my life, scatter, in Jesus' powerful Name.

Curses of Men: Blind Witches

By the power in the Blood of Jesus Christ, I *loose* myself from curses, spells, bewitchment, and idolatry, I loose myself from curses, spells, bewitchment, and idolatry of my father's house, in the Name of Jesus.

Everything that I have done to offend, insult, or interfere in anyone else's marriage, knowingly or unknowingly, Lord I repent; Lord, forgive me, wash me with the Blood of Jesus, Amen.

Curses of friends and fake friends and mouthy people: I break your power over me and my life, by the Power of the Lord's Christ.

I break every curse of *I give them a year,* regarding my marital life, in the Name of Jesus.

I break every word curse ever spoken against me, my Kingdom spouse, my marriage, my future, my destiny, in the Name of Jesus.

Lord, forgive me if I have ever knowingly or unknowingly cursed anyone, especially my own child or my own children.

Lord, if I'm a blind witch, a blind warlock, deliver me today, in the Name of Jesus.

Lord, anyone that I have wronged at any time in my life–, Lord, show Divine Mercy and hear my repentance, and forgive. Wash away all iniquity by the power in the Blood of Jesus.

If the person or people that I may have wronged is deceased, Lord have Mercy, Lord have Mercy, Son of David, have Mercy upon me, and forgive, in the Name of Jesus.

Lord, fulfill the covenant that You made with me according to Your Word. You are faithful and just; let the covenant of marriage be fulfilled in my life, in the Name of Jesus.

Let every curse against marriage, and in my life be broken now, in the Name of Jesus.

Lord, let the covenant of marriage be fulfilled in my life (x7), in the Name of Jesus.

Foundational problems siphoning off my blessings, be burned to ashes, in the Name of Jesus.

Prayers For a Godly Spouse

Mercy, draw divine connections to me, in the Name of Jesus. Mercy of God draw divine connections to me, in the Name of Jesus.

God, if I am two, where is the other one, in the Name of Jesus. Bring him/her to me, in Jesus' Name.

What God has joined together let no man tear it asunder, in the Name of Jesus.

The Word of the Lord shall prosper wherever He sends it, it shall not return to Him void.

Lord, help me to be prepared both spiritually, physically, emotionally, financially, naturally, in my proper, Godly marital role, in the Name of Jesus.

Lord, where I need more help preparing – give me the anointing to fulfill my marital roles and destiny, in the Name of Jesus.

Lord Jesus, call my Kingdom spouse to me, and me to my Kingdom spouse today, in the Name of Jesus.

Lord, make Your perfect will for my marriage plain to me, in the Name of Jesus.

Lord, bless me to do Your will and Your purpose now <u>and</u> after marriage, in the Name of Jesus.

Lord, if I am single, put my name on the Register of those who are available to be married.

Do not send any inappropriate suitors to me, in the Name of Jesus. Block every unacceptable, inappropriate suitor that the enemy may send, in the Name of Jesus.

In the Name of Jesus, Lord, I reject every adversary. I reject every enemy; Lord, send me a likeminded soul mate, not a roommate, a cellmate, or a jail mate, in the Name of Jesus.

Inherited idols, acquired idols in my soul that sponsor self-destruction, die, destroy yourself by the power in the Blood of Jesus.

Dark prophecies hovering over my destiny, be cut off by the power in the Blood of Jesus.

Any evil prophecy causing me to cry in secret, be silenced by the power in the Blood of Jesus.

Lord, send me a communicator, one who says what they mean, in truth and love and one who hears me when I speak, so that we are mutually respectful of one another. Amen.

Lord, clear my soul of distractions within me that cloud my ears and the same for my intended, in the Name of Jesus.

Lord, send me a suitor who wants to get married—someone likeminded, first having their mind on You and then on marriage, building, and fulfilling destiny, not someone I have to urge, or talk in to matrimony, in the Name of Jesus.

Tongue of confusion as a weapon in my relationship, backfire, in the Name of Jesus.

Lord Let me do no harm in my marriage and in parenting, and let me not be harmed in marriage, or parenting, in the Name of Jesus.

Marriage Deities

Lord, I repent of offending You with idolatry.

I renounce every love, lust, and marriage deity of every culture, worldwide, in the Name of Jesus. Lord, forgive me for serving any one of them in any way as a result of culture, tradition – without even thinking. Lord, forgive me for obeying **people** before I found out what Your Word says, in the Name of Jesus.

I repent of all the sins of ancestral idol worship in my bloodline, in the Name of Jesus.

Lord, I realize that anyone that I may have dated may have been serving idol *gods*, knowingly, or unknowingly. Just as you told Solomon not to marry those women because of the *gods they* worshipped, Lord, forgive me. I renounce any second-hand worship. Wash me with the Blood of Jesus so that it is not my undoing as it was for Solomon, in the Name of Jesus.

Any person who has rank in an idolatrous kingdom, keep them far away from me and me away from them; give me discernment to know, in the Name of Jesus.

Thank You Lord that an idolatrous person will not choose me, because his *idols* won't let him.

Lord God, block me from choosing an idolatrous spouse, in the Name of Jesus.

Lord, I list and request a divorce from any and every idolatrous marriage deity.

I request and ask issued a decree of divorce from every love or lust deity of my father's house, of my mother's house, even worldwide, in the Name of Jesus.

(Disclaimer: Speaking the names of the *gods* listed below, in no way invokes any of them, or constitutes worship to any of them. They are only named for the purpose of deliverance.)

Anansa, Baron La Croix, Baron Samedi, Erzulie Freda Dahomey, Oshun, Astarte, Bastet, Bes, Hathor, Min, Zamani, Inanna Ishtar, Nanaya, Aisha Qandicha, Prende, Milda, Dogoda, Dzydzilelya, Siebog, Živa, Lada, Jarilo, Venus, Áine, Branwen, Cliodhna, Babalon, Thelemic, Asmodeus, Eostre, Freyja, Frigg, Lofn, Sjöfn, Aphrodite, Dionysus,

Eos,Erotes, Anteros, Eros, Himeros, Hedylogos, Hermaphroditus, Hymen, Pothos, Hedone, Helios, Pan, Echo Syrinx. Diogenes of Sinope, Selene. Peitho, Philotes, Aurora, Eos, Bacchus, Dionysus, Cupid, Amor. Suadela, Venus, Albina, Turan, Astghik, Azrul, Kamadeva Rati, Ushas, Anahita, Aisyt, Bangan: Obban: Amas: Dian Masalanta: Alpriapo,Priapus, Mangagayuma, Agku, Tagbayaw, Jiutian Xuannü, Yue-Lao, Tu Er Shen, White Peony, Wutong Shen, Baimei Shen, Qian Keng (Peng Zu), Chuangmu, King Zhou, Daikokuten, Seven Lucky Gods. Ông Tơ Bà Nguyệt. Aizen Myō-ō or Rāgarāja, Kuni, Kurukulla, Ixcuiname, Teicu, Tiacapan, Tlaco, Tlazolteotl, Xocotzin, Xochiquetzal, Xochipilli, Kurupi, Rudá.

(Saints of God, you can see the above are names **not** to name your child.)

I ask for divorce from every love, beauty, lust, luxury, romance, or marriage deity listed above, and all that were left out, mispronounced or omitted, in the Name of Jesus.

I return and reject any thing proffered to me by any of them, I do not serve them, I do not worship them, I do not want them in my life, I break every soul tie with any of them, in the Name of Jesus.

I return all counterfeit inheritances from them, and receive my blessings and benefits only from the Lord Jesus Christ.

I enjoin any of those deities from punishing me for worshiping, or for not worshipping them, in Jesus' Name.
I repent of all the sins of ancestral idol worship in my bloodline, in the Name of Jesus. My marriage is not with or to the *gods* of my father's house.

Ancestral idols crying against my moving forward, be destroyed by Fire, in the Name of Jesus.

Any family *idol* still demanding my worship; I cut you off by the Blood of Jesus, in Jesus' Name.

I decommission every idolatrous requirement for marriage from my father's house,

I decommission every idolatrous requirement for marriage from my mother's house, in the Name of Jesus.

Powers punishing me for obedience and disobedience to ancient idols, Jesus Christ rebukes you; die, in the Name of Jesus.

Evil dedication of my life to the idols of my father's house, Blood of Jesus break, break now, in Jesus' Name.

All oppositions and oppression coming from the altars of the idols of my father's house, I challenge you with the power in the Blood of Jesus, DIE, in the Name of Jesus.

Idolatry in my foundation manifesting through food, alcohol, or drugs, die, in the Name of Jesus.

Idolatry in my blood manifesting through obedience to anti-Kingdom traditions and cultures, die, in the Name of Jesus.

Idols manipulating the message of Heaven in my mind, die to your own roots, in the Name of Jesus.

Holy Spirit, empower me to set boundaries against idolatrous agenda in my heart, in the Name of Jesus.

Battles of violated marriage rituals by my parents and ancestors--, for the sake of Christ release my marriage and let me fulfill destiny, in the Name of Jesus.

I release myself by the Blood of Jesus, from the curse of evil idols of my father's house, in the Name of Jesus.

Any strange personality in my family working against our destinies may God visit you by Fire, in Jesus' Name.

Jesus, you are the only one who can fix this. For the sake of Christ, Lord, release me now. Release me now. Release me now, in the Name of Jesus.

Agenda to have me never breakthrough until I perform a dark ritual, backfire, and let me fulfill destiny!

Agenda to have me never breakthrough until I bow before strange altars of my father's house or my mother's house, backfire, and let me fulfill destiny.

Agenda to have me never breakthrough until I worship family idols, even though I am in Christ, backfire, and let me fulfill destiny, in the Name of Jesus.

Agenda to have me never breakthrough until I visit dark rivers of my native place, backfire, in the Name of Jesus.

Agenda to have me never breakthrough until I obey family idols, backfire, and let me fulfill destiny, in the Name of Jesus.

Rites of passage all over the world are requirements of marriage; let all dark marriage rituals become powerless against me, in the Name of Jesus.

Lord, if my blood is shouting that I am not a woman, I am now in Christ, I silence that voice, with the Blood of Jesus.

If your blood is shouting that you are not a man, you are a man, you are now in Christ, silence that voice with the Blood of Jesus.

Battles

Battles of violated marriage rituals by my parents and ancestors, for the sake of Christ, release my sexual rights in marriage and let me fulfill destiny, in the Name of Jesus.

My sexual rights in the grip of darkness – I take it back, I take it back, I take it back, in the Name of Jesus.

Every manipulation of my sexual rights be normalized now, in the Name of Jesus.

Every unnatural decrease in libido, be corrected, in the Name of Jesus.

Every unnatural increase in libido, be corrected, in the Name of Jesus.

Sexual rights traders of my father's house, I am now in Christ, cease and desist!, in the Name of Jesus.

Sexual rights traders of my mother's house, I am now in Christ, cease and desist! in the Name of Jesus.

Wicked elders trading with my sexual rights let the covenant supporting you break, and release me, in the Name of Jesus.

Idols of my father's house with claims on my sexual rights, look at Christ, and DIE, in the Name of Jesus.

O Lord, let every helper-killer, helper-destroyer, helper-waster because of marriage and divine purpose, die out of my life!, in the Name of Jesus!

Marriage destroying agenda of offended *gods* of my father's house, backfire, in the Name of Jesus.

Marriage-destroying agenda of offended *gods* of my mother's house, backfire, in the Name of Jesus.

Breakthrough-destroying agenda of offended *gods* of my father's house, backfire, in the Name of Jesus.

Breakthrough-destroying agenda of offended *gods* of my mother's house, backfire, in the Name of Jesus.

I appropriate Christ. I am in Christ. I am fully in Christ, in the Name of Jesus.

Flesh and blood taking orders from darkness to afflict me, to kill me, die with darkness, in the Name of Jesus.

Flesh and blood taking orders from darkness to delay, stop, or destroy my marriage, cease, and desist; stand down, in the Name of Jesus.

Sexual rights – Lord, have any power that should not have any of my sexual rights release them now, so that I may fulfill marital destiny, in the Name of Jesus.

Whoever must give consent for me to be married, and it is not Jehovah God, let that power die, in the Name of Jesus. (x3)

Marriage is Holy unto the Lord.

Marriage is worship unto the Lord.

Goes into equals marriage. Lord, everyone I have ever *gone into or* has *gone into me,* that is not my kingdom spouse I ask for a decree of divorce in the Name of Jesus.

I repent and renounce the act; I break every evil covenant made in the process of that act, in the Name of Jesus.

Everything I gave away in the act, or afterward, or because of it, I take it back, I take it back, I take it back, in the Name of Jesus.

Every blessing, curse, promise, vow, oath – I undo it, disentangle it, unravel it and I take it back, in the Name of Jesus.

Everything stolen from me in the process that I didn't even know was part of the transaction, let it be returned to me today, immediately and 7-fold for my losses, in the Name of Jesus.

Release my sexual rights so I can have a legal, Kingdom spouse, to have relations without punishment, to enjoy my spouse, to enjoy my marriage, to be fruitful, multiply and bring forth righteous seed--, Lord, let it be. AMEN.

Lord, forgive me where I have put my sexual rights on display. Forgive me for masturbation in the Name of Jesus. Any wild bird that has run toward me for the seeds, let that power die.

Any *spirit spouse* that has insinuated itself into my life, let that *spirit spouse* die, in the Name of Jesus.

Any demon that has run toward me to form an evil soul tie, an evil covenant, even if that demon's name is *Nobody* – because nobody else was present, I break that covenant now. Come out, come up, come up and out of me now, in the Name of Jesus.

Lord, forgive me for strange fire, for spilled seed, for solo sex, in the Name of Jesus.

I cancel, I destroy, and kill anything created in the spirit because of solo sex; and because of it, I extract every part of my DNA from anything evil, synthetic, demonic, and unauthorized that was created by it because of trickery, ignorance, and disobedience, in the Name of Jesus.

Lord, let me observe the law of vows and keep every vow made to You, and made to one another in Your presence, to the utmost, in the Name of Jesus.

Any illicit sex, fornication, adultery, masturbation, bestiality, virtual sex, pornography ---that has created any evil spiritual marriage, I break those covenants now, in the Name of Jesus.

Lord, sex magic is witchcraft– by conjuring or agreeing with a demon – marrying them. Lord, forgive me, forgive me. Protect me from sex magic; Protect me from money rituals in the Name of Jesus.

Fantasy, role play – under any other name, its sex magic.

Lord, let any sexual experience of my youth where I gave away my sexual rights, Lord I repent of that behavior and renounce that behavior and I renounce the evil covenant formed because of it. Lord, in the Name of Jesus break that curse, and remove the demon sent to enforce that curse. As well, Lord, remove the iniquity formed because of it, in the Name of Jesus.

Lord, I break every soul tie formed from <u>every</u> sexual encounter, in the Name of Jesus.

Lord, if my first sexual experience wasn't approved by You, Lord, change me back, reset me to Your Godly standards, settings, affections, and proclivities, in the Name of Jesus – for purpose, for honor, and to the praise of Your Glory. Amen.

I break the desire for any sexual perversion, in the Name of Jesus. (X3)

Lord, where my sexual rights have been scattered—deliver me, gather them back for me, in the Name of Jesus.

Redeem My Star

Lord, my person's sexual rights are in my star. My marriage is in your star, my children and my family are in my star; Lord recover and uncover my Star, if it needs to be, in the Name of Jesus.

Lord, redeem my star from death, redeem my sexual rights, redeem my glory that I may have a Kingdom marriage and fulfill destiny, in the Name of Jesus.

Anyone who has taken my sexual rights without my permission; you are a thief and a liar – return my rights to me now, by the power in the Blood of Jesus.

Spirit of death because of misplaced, lost or stolen sexual rights – Pass over me, Pass over my house, Pass over my family and children, in the Name of Jesus.

Spirit of death because of adultery, Lord forgive and Pass over me, my household, in the Name of Jesus.

Spirit of death loosed because of heinous sexual sin, Lord, I repent.

Jesus, bind that *spirit* and have it pass over me and my household, by the Blood of Jesus.

Spirit of death because of <u>any</u> sin, Lord I repent; pass over me, in the Name of Jesus.

Polygamy

Lord, if by evil dedication I've been married off to some*thing* or someone…to take or tie up my sexual rights, Lord grant deliverance and divorce from every evil *spirit* marriage, in the Name of Jesus.

Lord, redeem me if I've been careless in my youth and lost my glory, my star, or my sexual rights--, redeem me, in the Name of Jesus, by the Blood of Jesus.

Lord, let me understand and put value on my sexual rights, in the Name of Jesus.

Promiscuity

Lord, forgive me for any and all promiscuity that scattered my seed and/or sexual rights.

Sex in the dream is random sex: whether it is forced promiscuity – with demons! Lord, deliver me from every evil power that wants to have relations with me, or has forced relations with me, in the Name of Jesus.

Lord, forgive me if I have sold my sexual rights for money, in the Name of Jesus.

Lord, forgive me if I have sold my sexual rights for **no money**, in the Name of Jesus. Lord, forgive me, cleanse me with the Blood of Jesus.

Lord, forgive me for playing the harlot, in the natural and in the spirit.

Forgive me for youthful lusts, ignorance, disobedience, rebellion.

Forgive me for being enticed in the most unlikely ways and in the most unlikely places, even in a church… by *alleged* saved people—some in leadership.

Lord, heal my foundation so I am not attractive to those people, (X2), in the Name of Jesus (x2).

Lord as you saved Rahab, save me--, save all who have played the harlot. I am now in Christ. (X2)

Like Lots daughters with good intentions, but deceived and ignorant—save me from my ignorance, in the Name of Jesus.

Lord, You are able to save to the utmost, You can save a Moabite and even a harlot--, save today, Lord, in the Name of Jesus.

Save today, Lord, so in ignorance we don't give worship to a demon or an idol *god*, such as Molech or Chemosh, in the Name of Jesus.

Cleanse me, Lord. Cleanse me, Lord. Cleanse me so I am worthy of a Kingdom spouse.
Cleanse my Kingdom spouse so that they are worthy of a Kingdom spouse.
Cleanse us both so we are worthy of a Kingdom marriage, in the Name of Jesus.

Lift Up Ye Gates

The Lord strong and mighty, the Lord mighty in battle, let the power of Your presence, cause all the gates, to lift up your heads. Gate of breakthrough, lift up your head. Gate of marriage and marriage success, lift up your head that the King of Glory can come in.

Requirement of entry to the Gate of my marriage that I cannot on my own fulfill, let the sacrifice of Christ pay for me. Lift up your head, o ye gates.

Powers at the gate of my next level breakthrough, you are robbers and destroyers, fall down and die, in the Name of Jesus.

Whatever strongmen are at the Gates of Marriage from my culture, traditions, bloodline, my place of birth, my place of residence, or origin—I bind that strongman and ask the Mighty angels of God to remove them from my Marital Gate, in the Name of Jesus.

Any power or entity that stands in the way of marriage, be defeated, in the Name of Jesus.

Let anything that belongs to the devil that is in my possession, my life or home, that is obstructing my marriage, receive Holy Ghost Fire, in the Name of Jesus.

Lord, let every anti-marriage weapon backfire, in the Name of Jesus.

Foundational strongmen blocking my marital gate, die, in the Name of Jesus.

I break every satanic stronghold in my life, in the Name of Jesus.

Anything planted in my doorpost to demote me, be neutralized by Holy Ghost Fire, in the Name of Jesus.

Generational yoke of sorrow, weeping, and disappointment in my foundation, be destroyed now, in the Name of Jesus.

Blood of Jesus, Holy Ghost Fire, purify my foundation, in the Name of Jesus. Any form of evil practices deeply rooted in my family, in my family's foundation, Fire of God, push it out, in the Name of Jesus.

Any power assigned to pull me down, I come against you by the unchallenged Name of Jesus Christ.

God of Elijah, arise in Your mighty power, and set me free from strange attacks and strange battles, in the Name of Jesus.

Any evil personality manipulating my life, confess and be exposed in Jesus' powerful Name.

Any strongman in my family that is keeping our breakthroughs in prisons, or strongrooms release them now by Fire, the King of Glory is coming in.

My family's glory! Hear the word of the Lord, appear by Fire, in Jesus' Name.

Envious Witchcraft

Envious witchcraft that causes people not to marry in my family, be dismantled, in the Name of Jesus.

Every evil wind directed at me to scatter what I am gathering, scatter, in the Name of Jesus.

O Lord, activate and restore Your miracles in my life and family, in the Name of Jesus.

I command you witchcraft of warlocks, witches, and wizards to remove your hands from my life now, by the power in the Blood of Jesus.

Any witchcraft rat, lizard, cat, or any other animal assigned to shut down my blessings, die by Fire, in Jesus' Name.

I divorce and/or break every plan of the devil that he has planned for me, in the Name of Jesus.

Lord, have Mercy: do not let me suffer for things that I did not know anything about in the past; I am in Christ now.

Idols in my soul taking worship by my suffering, die, by the power in the Blood of Jesus.

Serpent of the Lord that swallowed the serpents of the magicians of Egypt, swallow the ancient serpent of my father's house and let my deliverance appear, in the Name of Jesus.

Holy Spirit, You are the minister of Deliverance, deliver us from every deity of marriage, in the Name of Jesus.

Powers speaking when the Holy Spirit must speak, when Jesus Christ must speak, the Lord rebuke you, be quiet forever, in the Name of Jesus.

Powers speaking to me in the place of God, the Lord rebuke you, shut up and die out of my soul, in the Name of Jesus.

Any power that has taken my sexual rights, release my sexual rights, and die, in the Name of Jesus.

Any power that has stolen my sexual rights and believes it has married me--, DIE, in the Name of Jesus.

Jacob asked for sexual rights with Rachel; Lord have my Kingdom spouse follow the protocols of marriage and also ask You for permission to marry me, in the Name of Jesus.

Lord, let my Kingdom spouse have full possession of his own sexual rights, or have them not in the possession *or control of an idol *god*, in the Name of Jesus.

Whatever belongs to me, but I don't have because I violated a covenant, Blood of Jesus, pay for me so what is mine will be released, in the Name of Jesus.

Lord, let my Kingdom spouse follow the Godly rituals of marriage, so the marriage doesn't end up being the punishment, in the Name of Jesus.

I rebuke the *spirit of torment* in my marriage, in the Name of Jesus.

For my Kingdom marriage, Lord let me have Your direction, guidance, approval, and blessing, in the Name of Jesus.

For my Kingdom marriage, Lord, let me have my parent's or other spiritual authority in the Earth, let me have their approval and blessing, in the Name of Jesus.

These *gods* tormented my ancestors, my grandparents, my parents and they are now in line to torment me? Lord, cause that power to die, in the Name of Jesus.

Curse of illegitimate birth, break. Break against me. Curse of illegitimate birth, because of violated marriage ritual, break by the power in the Blood of Jesus.

I break every generational marriage curse in my family bloodline, in the Name of Jesus.

Lord, uncurse me, uncurse my marital destiny. Uncurse my ring finger. Uncurse me completely, in the Name of Jesus.

I am divorced from every idol *god* and *spirit spouse,* in the Name of Jesus.

I rid myself of every spirit child. I divorce *spirit spouse*, disentangle myself from every quantum entanglement in the Name of Jesus.

Lord, transfuse my blood with the Blood of Jesus. I am in Christ now. I am in Christ. I am in Christ.

Ancestral marriage violations, my own marriage violations Lord forgive me. If I have any iniquity coming because of interfering with anyone else's marriage, knowingly or unknowingly, Lord, forgive me, in the Name of Jesus. *If I am having trouble in marriage because of marriage sins of my ancestors, who may have interfered in other marriages, or worse --, Blood of Jesus cry me out of the iniquity, in the Name of Jesus.

Battles of offended *gods* in my life, die, by the power in the Blood of Jesus.

Battles of offended *gods* of love and marriage in my life, die, by the power in the Blood of Jesus.

Battles of offended *gods* in my life showing up as backward dreams, die by the power in the Blood of Jesus.

Powers/*idols* that used marriage to torment my parents and ancestors and you are still at work in my life? The Lord rebuke you, you are rebuked forever, in the Name of Jesus.

Battles that kicked my parents out of marriage and are still ongoing, die with your sponsors in my soul, by the power in the Blood of Jesus.

Battles that kicked my ancestors out of marriage and are still ongoing, die with your sponsors in my soul, by the power in the Blood of Jesus.

Any marriage punishment that I have coming, Lord, let the Blood of Jesus cry me out of it, in the Name of Jesus.

Not For the Streets

Every dark covenant sign or token I carry that will not allow me to be married, stay married, and be happily married, successful in marriage, let that token die, in the Name of Jesus.

If my dress code and dress preference is idol-inspired--, if it is for the streets, Jehovah the man of war, destroy the idols, and change my dress style, in the Name of Jesus.

Lord, have Mercy upon me:

Arise O Lord, judge the idols of my father's house.

Arise, O Lord, judge the idols of my mother's house.

Arise, O Lord, judge the idols of my place of birth.

Arise, O Lord, judge the idols of my residence.

Arise, O Lord, judge every idol against my marriage.

Arise, O Lord, judge every idol set against my destiny, in the Name of Jesus.

Water, air, and land, any territory made unavailable because of my disobedience or sin, become available by the power in the Blood of Jesus, and let my disobedience and sin in me die, in the Name of Jesus.

Lord, if I am in agreement with any of my destroyers and killers, I break the agreement, by the power in the Blood of Jesus. I break the agreement (x3), in the Name of Jesus.

Powers sitting in my soul and are not getting my worship, and you are punishing me because of it, die and let your punishment, backfire, in the Name of Jesus.

Powers in my soul that want to sit on my head so that I will not hear God, die, so that I will hear God, in the Name of Jesus.

Powers in my soul that sit on my head to block my brain, die, in the Name of Jesus.

STRANGE Woman/Strange Man

Anti-marriage and marital-failure curses sent against me, my family and bloodline, break, break, break, in the Name of Jesus.

Lips of the strange woman, or strange man, sweet as a honeycomb, lose your power, in the Name of Jesus.

Mouth of the strange woman, or strange man, smoother than oil, lose your power, in the Name of Jesus.

Steps of hell attached to the strange woman, or the strange man, I resist them by the power in the Blood of Jesus. Thunder Hammer of God, dismantle and tear up those steps. I resist Hell, I resist the pull of Hell, and any iniquity that draws me there, in the Name of Jesus.

Strange woman, strange man, lose your demonic charge against me, in the Name of Jesus.

Lord, whatever is in me that sees the strange woman or strange man, or would be attracted to it, Lord, have that *spirit* come up and out of me now, in the Name of Jesus.

Lord, I remove my feet from the door of the house of the strange woman or the strange man, in the Name of Jesus.

I anoint my threshold against the strange woman and the strange man; you are not welcome here, in the Name of Jesus.

Lord, give me the fruit of my own labor, and the power and the ability to keep it, and enjoy it--, that I do not give it, or my honor, my years to the cruel, to the evil, to the strange woman, or the strange man, or that it be found in the house of another, in the Name of Jesus.

Lord, let me love instruction. Let me love teachings. Let me Love Your Word, Love You, and love to do right, in the Name of Jesus.

Lord, I drink only from my own well, my own cistern, all the days of my Life. I drink pure waters, my own—not interspersed, comingled, or entangled with another, in the Name of Jesus.

Let me rejoice always with the Kingdom spouse that you have chosen and provided for me, Lord, in the Name of Jesus.

Let me rejoice always with the spouse of my youth, in Jesus' Name.

Let my spouse's love be pleasant and satisfy me at all times, in the Name of Jesus.

Lord, I reject every stranger, in the Name of Jesus.

Let me hear and obey every Holy Ghost ***Notificatio***n, in the Name of Jesus.

As from the time of my childhood, let me know and see stranger danger, even in dating, even in marriage, even in life, in the Name of Jesus. Amen.

Harlotry

I break the curse of confusion and I command the *spirit of confusion*, the *spirit of Babylon*, the harlot system, that nature, that flirtatious woman that goes after other *gods*, to release me, I command it to release me right now, in Jesus' Name.

I command any force, power, or entity that took away my self-worth and self-esteem to return it to me now, and then DIE, in the Name of Jesus.

I command the curse of evil, backbiting, slander, contention, anger, and hatred, to be broken off my life, now in Jesus' Name.

I command all sibling rivalry and household witchcraft to cease against me now, in the Name of Jesus.

I command good health for and in my Kingdom marriage.

I break the curse of:

- premature death,
- blood diseases and disorders,
- tumors,
- cancer,
- depression,
- insanity,
- arthritis,
- diabetes,
- hypertension,
- heart trouble,
- anxiety and any other disease and I command them to release me now, in Jesus' Name.

Lord, I decree, and I declare I am free in the Name of Jesus. Amen.

Ancestral Curses

Lord, break any curse that is on me for dishonoring father or mother, I repent of it in the Name of Jesus. I renounce and denounce that behavior. Lord, have Mercy upon me, remove the curse, in Jesus' Name.

Generational curses in my bloodline be destroyed by the Fire of the Holy Ghost, in the Name of Jesus.

I break the curse and bind the demon sent to enforce it, in the Name of Jesus. Lord, remove all iniquity.

Lord, break every generational curse in my family line, especially those of sexual immorality.

Lord, break all generational curses in my bloodline of addictions, alcohol, drugs, food, sex--, in the Name of Jesus.

Lord, break all generational curses in my bloodline of *pride* and *false humility*, in the Name of Jesus. Amen.

Break all generational curses of sickness and disease, division, and strife in our bloodline, in the Name of Jesus.

Lord, break all generational curses of witchcraft, divination, astrology, the occult, in the Name of Jesus.

Lord, I break all generational curses from abortion, sacrificing to Molech, in the Name of Jesus. Lord, forgive and cover with the Blood of Jesus.

Lord, break the curse of codependency and unhealthy interpersonal relationships, in my bloodline, in the Name of Jesus.

I break every curse operating in my family line by the Thunder Hammer of Jehovah God.

Lord let ancestral curses caused by mistakes of the parents, evil curses on the ancestors, polygamous inheritance, and repeated chronic afflictions, break, in the Name of Jesus.

Every ancestral curse causing demotion, delay, shame, hunger, debt, poverty, and marital delay, divorce, and sickness be broken by the power in the Blood of Jesus. Amen.

I break all barrenness off my life due to ancestral curses, or even my own sin, in the Name of Jesus.

I break every obstacle set up against my destiny due to any type of curse or spell, in the Name of Jesus.

Lord, let the voice of my Bloodline speak success, favor and good things for my life, in the Name of Jesus.

Break Family Curses

Lord, lay Your hands of protection upon me and my family, in the Name of Jesus.

Lord, close every dimensional access point that the enemy has to me, and my family, in the Name of Jesus.

Holy Ghost Fire, destroy every *monitoring spirit* and every monitoring device and gadget against me and my family, and business, in the Name of Jesus.

Lord, blot out the handwriting of ordinances that was against us, and nail it to the Cross of Jesus Christ Amen.

I break every family curse, every generational curse, ancestral curse, household curse, and marine curse, in the Name of Jesus.

I break all curses of anger, and bitterness in our family line, in the Name of Jesus.

I break every curse of unforgiveness, in the Name of Jesus.

Lord, I break the curse of anger off of me, especially if it is stopping me from becoming married in the Name of Jesus.

Lord, I break the curse of delay, in the Name of Jesus.

Lord, Jesus. In the Name of Jesus. Lord, break the curse that causes me to marry the wrong person.

Lord, I break every curse. That is in place to cause me to marry an evil person, such as a witch or warlock, in the Name of Jesus.

My blood, if you are drawing evil to me, as in a potential marriage partner, or a suitor, if you are drawing evil to me for any reason--, Blood of Jesus transfuse me, so I have the Blood of Jesus and no longer the blood of my ancestors, in the Name of Jesus.

Lord, in the Name of Jesus, I break every curse that is causing me to be noticed by the wrong person or the wrong type of person.

I break every curse that is causing me to be attracted to the wrong person or the wrong type of person, I break every curse that is causing me to become attached to the wrong person or the wrong type of person, in the Name of Jesus.

I curse the curse of sickness, illness, disease, disorder, any syndrome, symptoms--, anything that would cause me to not be well, or to be in a doctor's office or a sick bed, in the Name of Jesus.

Anything that would siphon money from my accounts in the Name of Jesus; I break every generational curse that is designed to drag me backward in life or to bring shame, disgrace, or the spoiling of reputation, in the Name of Jesus.

I break every curse that is designed to steal my dignity, or my progress and promotion, my willpower, my prayer life, or my spiritual gifts given by God, in the Name of Jesus.

Every ancestral curse attached to madness, depression, or confusion, be broken now, in the Name of Jesus.

Parental curses of the mother that have made me stagnant or limited, or rejected break, in the Name of Jesus.

Parental curses of the father that have made me stagnant, limited or rejected, break, in the Name of Jesus.

Curse of no destiny helper. Leave me now, in the Name of Jesus.

Curse of barrenness, break over my life, in the Name of Jesus.

Curse of aimless wandering break over me, in the Name of Jesus.

Father, send me a spouse who has a love for the home, balanced with travel and adventure and interest. Do not send a spouse whose feet cannot stay home, in the Name of Jesus.

Every curse of poverty, find your Sender, and backfire, sevenfold in the Name of Jesus.

Curse of restlessness in relationships—be destroyed in the Name of Jesus. Blessings of stability, peace, and cleaving be found in my marriage and in my home, in my life, in the Name of Jesus.

Any curse of hardship, sorrow, marital delay, or fruitless efforts break, in the Name of Jesus.

Curse of the polygamist family the polygamist home that has tormented my life--, do not find my children, in the Name of Jesus. Break now. I am in Christ.

Lord, if I'm under divine judgment. Have mercy upon me now in the Name of Jesus.

Remove the curse. Lord, I ask You, remove the curse. I repent and I renounce the sin and the transgression; Lord, please remove the curse in the Name of Jesus..

I plead the Blood of Jesus, I turn from my wicked ways and seek Your Face, Lord. Have Mercy on me.

Break Generational Curses:

Lord, I pray for protection for me and my family from every evil family curse sent to destroy our lives, or keep us from building a life together.

Father in Heaven, I pray that you break every evil yoke that the curses caused to be placed. Break them by Fire, Break them by Fire, Break them by Fire. Lord, destroy them and scatter them all in Jesus' Name.

Lord, deliver me from the fallout of the sins of my ancestors. Let me not reap the evil of their offences, in the Name of Jesus. Lord do not cause me to pay for something I did not buy, in the Name of Jesus.

Deliver me now, Father. I ask of you to please deliver me today from such curses.

Deliver my foundation so that I may fulfill destiny, especially as it concerns marriage, in the Name of Jesus.

Lord, deliver my children from all yokes placed on them by family curses. Free them today.

I break the power of every negative pronouncement (enchantment, curse, divination, spell and incantation) released upon me through evil foundation, in Name of Jesus.

Lord, turn away the curse afflicting my family. Turn that curse into generational blessings, in Jesus' Name.

I break and loose myself, from every collective evil covenant, in the Name of Jesus.

I command, the foundational strongmen attached to my family to die, in the Name of Jesus.

I release myself, from the curse of evil *idols* of my father's house, in the Name of Jesus..

Any strange power working against my family destiny, be wasted, in Jesus' Name.

Blood of Jesus Christ, Holy Ghost Fire, come in and break up every evil dedication and every evil altar, in the Name of Jesus.

Any part of my body handed over to Satan due to evil dedications, I take you back, in the Name of Jesus.

Holy Ghost Fire, break and destroy every destructive covenant operating in my life, in the Name of Jesus.

Blood of Jesus Christ, release me from the idols of my father's house, in the Name of Jesus.

By Holy Ghost Fire, I break and release myself from every covenant with idols of my fathers, house and my mother's house, in the Name of Jesus..

Oh Lord, release your Axe of Fire into my foundation and destroy every evil covenant speaking against me and my family, in the Name of Jesus.

I break and release myself from every evil covenant that my parents have put me in, in knowingly or unknowingly, in the Name of Jesus.

Blood of Jesus, break and release me from every blood and sexual covenant, in the Name of Jesus.

Holy Ghost Fire, Blood of Jesus, break and release me from every evil covenant operating between me and my place of birth, my place of residence and any place I've ever been or lived, in the Name of Jesus. Blood of Jesus, cover me, in the Name of Jesus.

Anyone among my siblings or my other relatives, or strangers, that my blessings have been given to, I retrieve them back to me now, in Jesus' Name.

All inherited infirmities and sicknesses in my body due to evil flow, dry up, in the Name of Jesus.

Break Covenants

Every curse issued on my head from my father's house; die in the Name of Jesus.

I release myself from the strongholds of my father's house in the Name of Jesus.

Any evil soul tie between me and my father; break by the Fire of the Holy Ghost.

Any evil soul tie between me and my mother; break by the Fire of the Holy Ghost.

I release myself from the dedication and covenants between me and the evil serpent of my Father's house, in the Name of Jesus.

Family taboos and idols crying against my breakthroughs, break by the Blood of Jesus.

Thunder Quake of God, destroy the ancestral prison holding me captive, in the Name of Jesus.

Poverty

Spirit of poverty afflicting me from birth, COME OUT and return to senders, in the Name of Jesus.

Blood of Jesus, deliver me from generational ancestral battles, in the Name of Jesus.

I refuse to be limited or share from the evil consequences in my lineage, in the Name of Jesus.

Lord, arise and attack every evil member attacking us with curses in the Name of Jesus.

Masturbation

Lord, do not let my marriage bed be defiled, in the Name of Jesus.

Lord, I know that solo sex is not solo, we are never alone. Lord let me always remember that and behave accordingly, in the Name of Jesus.

Lord, make me a helper fit for me. Make me fit for my Kingdom spouse, so there will be no unmet or auxiliary needs, in the Name of Jesus.

It is not good for man should be alone; Lord, thank You for making a helper that is fit for me, in the Name of Jesus. My beloved is mine, and I am his, in the Name of Jesus.

Thank You for the wonderful gift of God, which sex is. Gifts are for others, or else they are possessions.

Lord, Deliver me from porn if I need deliverance from it, in the Name of Jesus.

God of All Comfort, You have promised us satisfaction; let it be so, in the Name of Jesus, in our marital relationships.

Lord, in our Kingdom marriage, let us not be defrauded, or defraud our marriage partner, our Kingdom spouse, Amen.

Every evil arrow of sexual perversion or lust fired at me, DIE, in the Name of Jesus.

The *gods* of my father's house causing perversion, intense or constant sexual appetite in me, DIE, in the Name of Jesus.

The *gods* of my father's house that have taken my sexual appetite, DIE in the Name of Jesus.

Holy Ghost, locate and destroy any *spirit spouse* that has sexually violated me, in the dream, in the sleep, in the Name of Jesus. Kill 'em! in the Name of Jesus.

Holy Spirit undo every emotional relationship of the past that has my soul tied in any way, in the Name of Jesus.

Every spirit marriage that is blocking marriage in the physical, DIE, in the Name of Jesus.

Transactions of my conception that set me up for sexual sins in my life, be undone by the power in the Blood of Jesus.

Lord, if my parents were freaks, don't let that have transferred to me, or to my children, through me, in the Name of Jesus.

Every sexual marriage by *spirit spouse* to have a basis to sexually violate me, and or steal my sexual rights, DIE in the Name of Jesus.

Assignment given to me by *spirit spouse* of my mother's or father's house – so that I do not leave or cleave, die, in the Name of Jesus..

Any poison tongue that has issued curses over others, let that tongue be silenced, in the Name of Jesus.

Let those curses fall to the ground and die, and come to nothing. Let them fall to the ground as dead works, in the Name of Jesus.

Lord, in the Name of Jesus. I reverse every curse against me and my family. And those that cannot be reversed, Lord, I receive your deliverance now in the Name of Jesus.

Any strange curse issued against me or my family backfire! Back to sender, in the Name of Jesus.

Lord, by praying these prayers, especially the prayers for my foundation, I pray for the marriage, successful marriage of my children also, and their children to 1000 generations in my bloodline, in the Name of Jesus.

Now Lord, that these curses have been broken and destroyed before Your Courtroom, I pray for the speedy release of my Godly Kingdom spouse and no further delays in marriage, in the Name of Jesus.

Lord, let every frustration, disappointment, and loss – including the loss of time, joy, peace, happiness, love, prosperity, and children—that this satanic curse has taken from me, be restored.

Everything withheld or stolen from me be returned to me at least 7-fold, in the Name of Jesus.

Lord, let our marital blessings locate me now, in the Name of Jesus.

Nearly Married Syndrome

Lord, marriage is a divine appointment. Lord let me keep every divine connection and divine appointment You have set for my life, in the Name of Jesus.

Lord, in our own timeline, and keep me in purpose. Divine Purpose fight for me, for my marriage and my children, in the Name of Jesus.

I cover myself with the Blood of Jesus and I ask for mighty warrior angels for protection, in the Name of Jesus.

Holy Ghost Fire destroy the foundation of delay and failure in my life, in Jesus' Name.

God arise and expose the evil personality waging war against my marriage and marital destiny, in Jesus' Name.

Lord, kill every *spirit spouse*, by Fire, in the Name of Jesus.

I break the power of all curses, vexes, spells, hexes, charms, fetishes, psychic prayers, psychic directions and thoughts, all sorcery, incantations, chanting, blessings, hoodoo, witchcraft, voodoo, magic, all mind control, potions, jinxes, bewitchments, death, destruction, torment, psychic power, psychic warfare, sickness, pain, evil prayer chains, incense, and candle burning and everything else being sent to me or my family member's way, or any deliverance ministries way. I rebuke and return the demons to the sender sevenfold. I bind them by the power of Jesus, and I cut and burn their ungodly silver cord and ley lines, in Jesus' powerful and mighty Name.

I break every curse of the wanderer and the vagabond from my life and my family's lives in the Name of Jesus.

I break the curse of disobedience, rebellion and not obeying the Word of the Lord.

I command selfishness and greed to leave me; release me in Jesus' mighty Name.

I break all curses off my fields, lands and inheritance in Jesus' Name.

I command all rebellion operating in my bloodline to cease in Jesus' powerful Name.

Stubborn curses attacking me at the edge of my breakthrough, break by Fire, in Jesus' mighty Name.

By the power of the Holy Spirit, I am delivered from every financial, spiritual, social, or psychological bondage, in Jesus' Name.

I set myself free from bondages to failure, sickness, poverty, untimely death, retrogression, lack and failure at the edge of success, in Jesus' Name.

I break and scatter every curse of marital delay affecting me and affecting the family, in Jesus' Name.

Afford To Get Married

Lord, You give us the Power to get wealth so that You may establish covenant with us. Father, send forth prosperity: we want to establish covenant with our Kingdom spouse, in the Name of Jesus.

Lord, let us afford to get married, stay married, and be happy in marriage, in the Name of Jesus.

Lord, hear our prayers for financial breakthrough, in the Name of Jesus.

Altars of generational poverty operating in my lineage, be wiped off by the Blood of Jesus.

Every curse of poverty upon my family line due to evil covenants, break and die, in the Name of Jesus.

Witchcraft curses of untimely death and poverty upon my life, break and die, in the mighty Name of Jesus Christ.

Witchcraft curses of hardship upon my life, break, and scatter, by Jesus' Name. Any part of my destiny arrested by witchcraft receive power of God and come alive now, in Jesus' Name.

Lord Jesus, let blessings and favor locate me anywhere, and everywhere I go, in Jesus' Name.

Any witchcraft power that has stolen from me, in the dream, be arrested now, in the Name of Jesus.

Lord don't make me pay for things I didn't know anything about, and I didn't buy.

Lord, don't make me pay for things that I didn't buy, didn't use, didn't get the benefit of in the Name of Jesus.

Lord, don't make me pay for things just because of my blood, in the Name of Jesus.

Lord, please bless me abundantly so that no family curse on poverty is able to ruin our marital destiny, in the Name of Jesus..

Every evil wind directed at me to scatter what I am gathering, you scatter, by the East Wind of God, in the Name of Jesus.

God, please bless me abundantly so that no family curse of poverty that is trying to make me poor will succeed in Jesus' Name.

Lord in Heaven, every curse causing financial problems in my life right now, deliver me from such, deliver from those curses now and forever Amen.

Lord, restore my financial glory today in the Name of Jesus.

My Father I ask for Your Grace to overcome all obstacles that might come my way due to ancestral curses and consequences of the same, in the Name of Jesus.

Witchcraft curses attacking me at the edge of breakthrough, break by Fire, in Jesus' Name.

Every stronghold attached to my breakthroughs, I bind you, in Jesus' Name.

I command crashlanding of witches and wizards assigned against my breakthroughs, in the Name of Jesus.

Lord in Heaven, curse every financial problem in my life right now, deliver me from such curses now and forever, and restore my financial glory today in Jesus' Name.

God in Heaven, I ask for Your help in my family life. Grant us prosperity, and victory over all sicknesses, diseases, and disorders.

Lord, whatever ancestral curses that the enemy may have laid on my family preventing us from soaring high financially, break those, in the Name of Jesus. Amen.

My head reject every word of misfortune, failure and stagnation in the Name of Jesus.

Altars of generational poverty operating in my lineage, be wiped off by the Blood of Jesus.

I break and release myself from every form of inherited poverty and sickness, in Jesus' Name.

Every evil power assigned against the prosperity, fruitfulness, success, promotion, progress, and breakthrough of my family, from my mother's side or from my father's side, through marriage, and is against me in any way because of my blood, be destroyed, in the mighty Name of Jesus Christ.

Every arrow of affliction fired to my life to waste my time and money, backfire, in the Name of Jesus.

Hosts of Heaven, I call on You this day; deliver my children from all yokes placed on them by family curses. Set them free today, in the Name of Jesus.

My Father, my God, come to my rescue and help me to break these curses totally, in Jesus' Name. I declare that they shall not holdover into my children's lives, and into my generations, in the Name of Jesus.

Lord, You delivered Shadrach, Meshach and Abednego from the burning furnace. I call on You today, deliver me as you delivered them from all of these problems, in the Name of Jesus.

I break and release myself from every form of inherited poverty and sickness, in Jesus' Name.

Powers that have vowed to make sure I remain at the level where I am, right now be wasted by Fire, in Jesus' Name.

Father, grant us prosperity and victory over all sicknesses/ diseases.

Whatever ancestral curse that the enemy has put on my family preventing us from financial successes, I break all of those, in Jesus' mighty Name.

Break Curses Over My Children

I cover my children, born and unborn, with the Blood of Jesus, in Jesus' Name.

Father, cancel every curse on the heads of my children, in Jesus' Name.

Any curse has been issued on my children--, I break them in Jesus' Name.

I separate my children from all evil foundations, in the Name of Jesus.

Any family or generational curse because of my ancestors, because of the ancestors on either side, of my children, in the Name of Jesus, I separate them from it, in the Name of Jesus.

I release my children from every ancestral curse, in the Name of Jesus, I release my children from any Curse of the polygamous woman, the rolling stone/polygamous man, or from the polygamous marriage, in the Name of Jesus.

Power of my father's house, release the glory of my children, in the Name of Jesus.

I break and scatter every evil curse, and every evil covenant working against my children, in Jesus' Name.

Any problem that's coming to my children's life because of my mistakes. Lord, I repent of those mistakes, and I denounce them, I renounce and denounce them, in the Name of Jesus.

Lord, let my children receive a *spirit of respect* and boldness. And let them resist every negative fear, every irrational fear, in the Name of Jesus.

I withdraw my name, the names of my children, from the Book of Death, in the Name of Jesus.

My children will not answer the call of Death, in the Name of Jesus.

My children will not answer the calling of their name by any strange powers or voices, in the Name of Jesus.

Lord, let my children be able to hear You from an early age.

Any witch or wizard that is after the life of my children be roasted by Fire, in the Name of Jesus.

Any infection or disease in the bodies of my children, be cleansed by the Blood of Jesus.

Any poison eaten by my children in the dream or in the natural, be neutralized by the power in the Blood of Jesus.

Lord, let the agenda of the enemy concerning my children scatter into desolation, in the Name of Jesus.

Any power holding back my children's stars or glory break! in the Name of Jesus.

Lord, I refuse to work against the destiny of my own children in Jesus' Name. I refuse to leave them debt of any kind--, not spiritual debt, natural debt, financial debt, emotional debt--, debt of any kind, in the Name of Jesus, my the Blood of Jesus.

Lord, silence my foundation from trouble in the destiny of my children, in the Name of Jesus.

I release my children from every ancestral curse from any strange, polygamous woman, in Jesus' Name.

Power of my father's house; release the glory of my children, in Jesus' Name.

Every link between my children and any evil foundation, break, scatter, and die, in Jesus' Name.

I break and scatter any evil curses and covenant working against my children, in Jesus' Name.

Any problem that came into my children's life through my mistakes, I nullify all the effects of the same, in the Name of Jesus.

I cover my children's lives with the Blood of Jesus, in Jesus' Name. Thank You, Lord. Thank You, Jesus.

Evil yokes holding back the stars of my children, break, in the Name of Jesus.

I refuse to leave my children in debt, in Jesus' Name.

Every serpent in my life determined to waste the destiny of my children due to envy and jealousy, roast by Fire, in the Name of Jesus.

Blood of Jesus silence any *spirit* from my foundation troubling my children's destiny, in Jesus' Name.

Father, in the Name of Jesus as a parent, allow me, give me the Grace and the anointing and the ability and Wisdom to protect my child's sexual rights until they are ready to get married.

Lord, give me the Wisdom, Grace and anointing to do that, in the Name of Jesus.

Parents acknowledge that teens are wrestling with sexual sin and masturbation, in the Name of Jesus. May the Lord grant you Wisdom to address that and to be victorious over it, in the Name of Jesus.

Parents protect your children until they can protect themselves.

Protect your child's sexual rights until they are ready to be married.

Heal the Land

Father, in the Name of Jesus, if I am living in a house where the foundation is cursed, deliver me, and deliver this land, and this house, in the Name of Jesus.

Lord, heal the land of my marriage, in the Name of Jesus.

I receive the power of God to move forward in every area of my life, in the Name of Jesus Christ.

I decree total deliverance upon my life, upon my spouse upon my children, upon my siblings, upon my parents, in the mighty Name of Jesus Christ.

Any power that has put a curse on my marriage – it's duration, it's quality--, I break that curse and I declare that this covenant, my covenant with the Most High God overrides that curse, and we shall be married as long as we both shall live, and we can live until we are satisfied, as God gives us length of days, long life, and satisfaction, in the Name of Jesus.

I shall not die but live to fulfil my God-given destiny and my marital destiny, in Jesus' Name.

Lord, I thank You.

Lord, I bless You, that we are able to come into Your Courts, and by Your Mercy You've heard our prayers and You've extended Your power to our decrees, declarations, and judgments, in the Name of Jesus.

Thank You Lord. I bless You because You alone are God, and there is none like You.

I cover all these prayers, these decrees and declarations with the Blood of Jesus.

I seal these declarations, across every age, realm and era, and timeline from now to infinity. I seal them with the Blood of Jesus and the Holy Spirit of Promise, in the Name of Jesus.

Any attacks because of these prayers, backfire against the enemy and the sender 7X, in the Name of Jesus.

We bless You, Lord; we Thank You and we count it all as done, in the Name of Jesus. **Amen.**

Dear Reader

Thank you, dear reader for acquiring and reading this volume. May it make a difference in your life. May your marriage be a Kingdom marriage, may it last and you be happy and successful with kingdom children. Let your salvation be worked out and may your entrance into the Gates of Heaven, at the appointed time, be glorious.

Until then, honor God every day of your life, in the Name of Jesus.

Amen.

Dr. Marlene Miles

Other books by this author

AK: The Adventures of the Agape Kid

AMONG SOME THIEVES

Ancestral Powers

Battlefield of Marriage (The)

Blindsided: *Has the Old Man Bewitched You?*

https://a.co/d/5O2fLLR

Churchzilla, The Wanna-Be, Supposed-to-be Bride of Christ

Demons Hate Questions

Devil Weapons: Unforgiveness, Bitterness,...

Dream Defilement

Don't Refuse Me, Lord (4 book series)

Every Evil Bird

Evil Touch

Fantasy Spirit Spouse

FAT Demons (The): *Breaking Demonic Curses*

The Fold (5 book series)

The Fold (Book 1)

Name Your Seed (Book 2)

The Poor Attitudes of Money (3)

Do Not Orphan Your Seed (4)

For the Sake of the Gospel (5)

Gates of Thanksgiving

got HEALING? Verses for Life

got LOVE? Verses for Life
https://a.co/d/57a4Ob8

got HOPE? Verses for Life

got money?

How to Dental Assist

How to Dental Assit2: Be Productive, Not Wasteful

Let Me Have A Dollar's Worth

Living for the NOW of God

Lose My Location https://a.co/d/crD6mV9

Man Safari, *The* (mini book from Wilderness Romance)

Marriage Ed. Rules of Engagement & Marriage https://a.co/d/0wT7aCb

Made Perfect in Love https://a.co/d/963aSGF

Motherboard (The) - soul prosperity series

Plantation Souls

Power Money: Nine Times the Tithe

The Power of Wealth *(forthcoming)*

Seasons of Grief

Seasons of War

Second Marriage, Third Marriage, Any Marriage
https://a.co/d/1AkaaCr

Sift You Like Wheat

Soul Prosperity soul prosperity series 3

https://a.co/d/5p8YvCN

Souls Captivity soul prosperity series 2

The Spirit of Poverty

This Is NOT That: How to Keep Demons from Coming At You

Throne of Grace: Courtroom Prayer

Time Is of the Essence

Too Many Wives: *Why You Have Lady Problems*

https://a.co/d/gVr3R6H

Tormenting Spirits https://a.co/d/dAogEJf

Triangular Power *(series)*

Powers Above

SUNBLOCK

Do Not Swear by the Moon

STARSTRUCK

Uncontested Doom

Upgrade: How to Get Out of Survival Mode

Toxic Souls (Book 2 of series)

Legacy (Book 3 of series)

Warfare Prayer Against Beauty Curses

Warfare Prayer Against Poverty

What Have You to Declare?

When the Devourer is Rebuked

The Wilderness Romance *(series)*

- *The Social Wilderness*
- *The Sexual Wilderness*
- *The Spiritual Wilderness*

Credits

Inspired by: **Courtroom Prayers for Marriage** by Pius Joseph https://a.co/d/ev3xcKw

Evil Spiritual Marriage by Dr. Anthony O. Akerele, https://a.co/d/bjlrmO8

Marriage Ed., Rules of Engagement and Marriage by this author. https://a.co/d/i0hFiqb

Some prayer points from or adapted from:

Minister Joshua Orekhie

Wikipedia https://en.wikipedia.org/wiki/List_of_love_and_lust_deities

Notes

www.ingramcontent.com/pod-product-compliance
Lightning Source LLC
LaVergne TN
LVHW010936110826
845149LV00013B/2625

* 9 7 8 1 9 6 3 1 6 4 0 7 7 *